MANCHESTER AS IT WAS

by

CHRIS. MAKEPEACE, B.A., A.L.A.

Volume III   *Social and industrial life* — A look at the living and working conditions of the less well off members of society, what was done to help them by organisations, what they did in their spare time, always assuming they had any.

Cover picture: Long Millgate — one of the oldest streets in Manchester was a mixture of both shops and business premises. It was a road which linked the Market Place and the Cathedral with the slums of Red Bank and Angel Meadow. The photograph was taken around 1895.

Published by: Hendon Publishing Co., Hendon Mill, Nelson, Lancs.

Text: © Chris. Makepeace, 1974.

Printed by: Turner & Earnshaw Ltd., Bread Street, Burnley, Lancs.

93p

INTRODUCTION

Behind the facades of wealth and prosperity in Victorian Manchester, there lay another world — the world of the workers and the less fortunate for whom life was often hard and at times brutal. The gulf between the two sections of society was deep, but not impassable for anyone prepared to work very hard and had more than his fair share of good fortune. For working men and women, their main concern was to earn enough money to pay for their daily requirements and if money ran short, there was always the pawnshop around the corner where some treasured possession could be pawned for a few shillings to be redeemed on payday. In times of economic boom, jobs were safe and money more plentiful, but during trade slumps, unemployment was a very real threat and this brought the spectre of starvation, begging and even the workhouse looming over their lives. This third volume of "Manchester as it was" looks at some aspects of life in Victorian Manchester that were less frequently recorded by the photographers as it showed the less pleasant side of life. Authors and social commentators had written and reported on social conditions since the early 19th century and societies were formed to promote the various views put forward. It was not, however, until the last decade of the 19th century that photographs were used to illustrate annual reports of organisations involved in social work. One of the first bodies to do this was the Manchester and Salford Methodist Mission who first used photographs in the middle of the decade to reinforce and illustrate the points they made in the annual reports.

Many of the photographs in this volume have come from the photographic collection housed in Manchester Public Library's Local History Department which has been built up over many years through the generosity of people giving photographs they did not want to the Library. Our gratitude is also due to the many photographers who took the pictures used and through whose persistence and work such collections have been made possible and our knowledge of life in Victorian Manchester increased. Anyone who has photographs or postcards of Manchester, the Local History Department at Manchester Central Library would be interested in borrowing them to be copied. Alternatively, if I am contacted at my home address, 27, Eastleigh Road, Heald Green, Cheadle, Cheshire, I can arrange for copies to be made and the originals returned.

I must thank Mr. D. Taylor and Miss R. Morris for their assistance and advice when making the initial selection of photographs and the staff of the Local History Library for their assistance and patience whilst I was checking details. I should also like to thank Mr. D. I. Colley, Director of Culture for Manchester for permission to use the photographs from the Local History Library, from where a majority of the photographs have come. Thanks are also due for permission to reproduce the following photographs: Dr. R. L. Hills of the North Western Museum of Science and Industry for the photographs on pages 14 and 15; Miss J. Aytoun for the lower photograph on page 5; Mrs. M. Bellhouse for the upper picture on page 17; Mrs. Bellicon for the top right hand photograph on page 41; Miss Crossley for the upper photograph on page 5; Mr. R. Dunning for the photograph on page 9; the Lancashire and Cheshire Temperance Union for the lower photograph on page 40; the Manchester and Salford Methodist Mission for the photographs from their annual reports; Mr. A. J. Pass for the photograph on page 22, Dame M. Tylecote for the photograph on page 33 and the lower one on page 41 and Wood St. Mission for the photographs on page 4. Thanks are also due to Miss Gillian Howarth who kindly read through the manuscript and made many helpful suggestions. Finally, my wife, Hilary, for her help and encouragement whilst working on this volume.

Children born into families who lived in the densely populated areas of inner Manchester did not have the best introduction to life. Their world was one of rows of mean, terraced houses in a smoky environment with few trees or plants and even fewer parks and playgrounds. The playground for many children was not the backyard, as few houses had one of any size, but the streets around their homes. The three boys in the lower right hand photograph appear to be contented with their position despite their lack of toys and amenities. Their clothing would horrify child care officers of the 1970s and their lack of footwear would be treated as a scandal. The three boys sharing either some food or a home made toy were probably more contented than children with many expensive toys and ideal surroundings.

Roaming the streets, children would get thirsty, but in some areas there were to be found drinking fountains. These had been mainly erected in the 1860s when town councils and others who wished to be regarded as philanthropic had had the fountains erected at strategic points throughout the city to supply fresh water supplies. The photograph at the top left shows a boy using the fountain that had been erected at Bank Top near where London Rd. Station was located.

For most of the 19th century, there was a distinct lack of public facilities where children could play, free from the thread of road traffic and annoying the neighbours. In 1868 swings had been erected on the Flags at Angel Meadow, but Ancoats had to wait almost 30 years before such facilities arrived. The photograph at the top right shows a children's playground at Jersey St. where the children were able to play under the superintendance of members of the staff of the Manchester & Salford Methodist Mission.

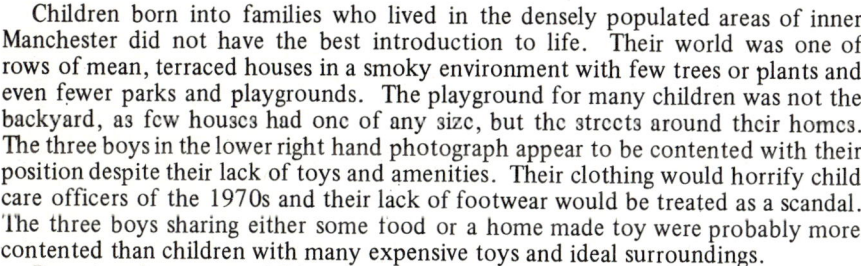

3

During the 19th century legislation was introduced which regulated the employment of children in mills, factories and mines, but nothing was done concerning the treatment of children in their own homes. However, progress was made in the field of child care, but it was not due to the work of the state, but to that many individual philanthropists like Alfred Alsop. In 1869, Alsop and a few friends began to hold street services in Lombard Street, off Deansgate. Shortly afterwards he opened a mission in the area, which was described by the local police as "the rendezvous of thieves and a very hot bed of social iniquity and vice". In 1873, Alsop moved the mission to new premises in Wood Street and attempts were made to combat the poverty and wretchedness that was to be found in the surrounding area. Soup Kitchens were established, toys distributed to needy children at Christmas and deserving families received gifts of clothing and footwear. Boys who were discovered sleeping rough were taken to the Mission and efforts made to find them a permanent job or assist them to emigrate, usually to Canada to start a new life.

Many children from the Manchester slums never saw the countryside or seaside during the 19th century until the various organisations devoted to child welfare began organising seaside trips. These were extremely popular as the top photographs show with boys (left) and girls (right) queue outside Wood Street for their place on the trip. The Boys and Girls Refuges in Strangeways organised their first camp for boys at Morecambe in 1883 when 48 boys attended. Ten years later over 1120 boys went to the camp at Ainsdale and the success of such ventures was assured. The lower photograph shows a party from Wood Street on the beach at Birkdale after having sampled the delights of sea-bathing.

When Manchester Grammar School was founded in 1515, it was intended that there should be no fees charged to parents of boys who attended. The necessary finance was obtained from the monopoly the school enjoyed in the field of grinding grain first for bread and later for malt. The income from this source was sufficient to enable the school to maintain its position as Manchester Free Grammar School until the middle of the 19th century when the income of the mills declined and in order to continue in existence, a more suitable basis for the school's finances had to be found. It was decided that the only way this could be achieved was to introduce the principle of fee paying and the school changed its name to Manchester Grammar School. At the same time, the need for enlarged building arose and during the 1860's these were constructed on the school's site on Long Millgate. The photograph on the left shows the gymnasium at the Grammar School near the end of the 19th century with its equipment that would be the envy of the other schools in Manchester. Note the regimental way the boys are lined up for the photographer, a feature which was symptomatic of the rigid discipline that existed in all schools at that time.

The 1870 Education Act introduced compulsory education for all children although it was not free every child having to pay a small sum. The schools were run by an elected body called the School Board, who were also supposed to build new schools. Initially, voluntary schools were handed over to the Board and it was not until 1874 that the first board school was opened — Vine Street in Hulme. The photograph shows a typical school class at a school in east Manchester — Culceth British School in 1895. The dress of the children is typical of that of the period before they left and went out to work. When the children left school, they had to reach a certain standard and obtain a certificate to show that they had attained this level otherwise both the parents and the employers could be asked to explain before the School Board.

A town with a rapidly expanding population has, amongst its many other problems, that of finding adequate housing for the newcomers. Houses which would have been condemned as unfit and cleared away many years before continued to stand and be occupied whilst new property was erected as quickly and as cheaply as possible, resulting in the creation of slum areas. Social commentators wrote extensively on the subject of bad housing and the effects it had on the population's health from the 1830's onwards, but photographers did not capture the scene until considerably later and local authorities only reluctantly became involved in the problems of bad housing and clearance. The photograph above shows a little area off Red Bank, near the River Irk, called Gibraltar. The buildings, erected around 1668, were in their final stages of decay when James Mudd captured the scene around 1877. Although derelict looking and no residents listed in the directories, the presence of a hand-cart and the "ghost" of a man indicate that someone had found some use for the property. It was the gradual decay of areas such as Gibraltar that prompted members of Manchester Amateur Photographic Society to take an interest in the scenes and buildings they saw around them especially those which were threatened with demolition and to record them for posterity. This interest, incidentally, is still maintained by the Society to this day with their Photographic Record Section.

Older property in the centre of Manchester gradually disappeared, but in the suburbs such property continued to exist well into the 20th century. Cottages similar to the ones shown above could be found in many parts of the outer Manchester area and were inhabited by people of a variety of professions. The row of cottages shown above were at the corner of Burnage Lane and Fog Lane and were erected in the first years of the 19th century. They continued to stand until about 1928 when they were demolished to make way for a housing estate. It is possible to trace who was living in the cottages at a specific time. For example in 1900 the residents were as follows (starting at the corner with Burnage Lane): George Beasely, labourer; William Hodgkinson, shoemaker; Samuel Axon, wheelwright; Thomas Yates, gardener and Thomas Dearn, labourer. Although several miles out of the centre of Manchester, the street had gas lighting. The gas was supplied by Manchester Corporation who had started gas production in 1817 and charged 14/- per 1000 cubic feet. Manchester's gas works gradually extended its supply to the suburbs although the suburbs that were independent at that time had to pay extra for the gas supplies. For example, Crumpsall was charged 3/2d per 1000 cubic feet plus £300 a year for pipes and maintenance. The importance gas assumed in the 19th century can be shown by the fact that gas consumption rose from 248m cu.ft. in 1843 to 5000m cu.ft. in 1899 and the profits the Gas Department made went to keeping the rates down.

The worst areas of housing that were to be found in 19th century Manchester were the parts of the city that were constructed during the opening decades of the 19th century on the eastern fringes of what is now the central area of Manchester. The population at this time had increased very rapidly and there was an unsatisfied demand for new property. Between 1773 and 1871, the population of Manchester rose from an estimated 22,481 to 353,655. The first forty years of the 19th century saw the greatest rise in the population from 75,272 in 1801 to 253,162 in 1841 and the population of the township of Manchester rose by 750% in this 40 year period. Cheapness and speed were essential in the construction of new houses and as many as possible were crammed into each acre developed. Back-to-back houses, courts, and terraced houses were built to accommodate the rising population with cellar dwellings being amongst the worst that existed. There is little wonder that diseases like cholera and typhoid flourished in houses that had no running water and proper sanitation. In 1844 Manchester Corporation made some attempt to bring the situation under control by inserting in the Police Act that was passed for the town certain clauses which laid down standards of toilet provision both in the home and in places of work. This was, however, only the first step on a long road to providing adequate sanitary and housing conditions in the city. The photographs show some of the property that existed in late 19th century Manchester. The top right photograph shows property in Long Millgate, some of the courts are shown on the top right and back-to-back houses on the bottom right.

In 1868, Manchester Corporation established a Health Department amongst whose duties was that of dealing with unfit housing and improving conditions under which people lived. The Police Act of 1844 had laid down the minimum sanitary provisions and abolished the erection of back-to-back houses, but as Manchester extended its boundaries, it took over areas where such provisions had not existed so there was always a backlog of work to be done. The first target for the Health Department was to abolish cellar dwellings within the city. Between 1868 and 1872, over 2,400 cellars were closed and in 1874 it was claimed there were only 108 cellars still inhabited and these by elderly people who were being rehoused as soon as was possible. Although the Health Department wanted to improve living conditions, their activities were hampered by the lack of land on which to build new houses whilst the old ones were cleared. One commentator wrote that "the exigencies of commerce have done more to sweep away the old fever dens of Manchester than could have been accomplished within the same period by any requirement of sanitary legislation". For example, the construction of the Cheshire Lines Railway into Central Station resulted in the reduction by 50% of the population of St. Matthew's parish and the destruction of much slum property. In 1889, Dr. Thresh of Ancoats wrote of the housing of Ancoats: "These blocks of insanitary buildings must be removed from their very foundations". The Corporation responded by organising a competition to design a tenement block — for workers. The competition was won by Spalding and Cross who had had previous experience of such work. The block was described as being as "of fair, average character, light and airy, every tenement having a toilet". This description is interesting as Spalding is reported to have been reactionary in his views on working class housing claiming that it was necessary to build houses to standards to which "working classes are accustomed" or else "we shall find the class of people for whom we intend to provide will not live inour building". At street level there were shops intended to replace those demolished when the block, known as Victoria Square and shown above was erected. Other tenement blocks did exist in Manchester, some were specifically designed as such, but others were converted from other buildings. The most interesting of these was Jersey Street Dwellings which was converted into dwellings from a cotton mill in 1892. The flats had three rooms with running water in the living room although there was no individual toilet facilities. These flats continued to be occupied until 1940 when the size of the building was considered to be a prize target for German bombers and the remaining residents rehoused.

Around the city of Manchester during the 19th century were to be found the remnants of a by-gone age when agriculture played a much larger part in the economy of the area than it did in Victorian times. These remnants were the old farm houses, many of which were called halls, presumably because of their size in comparison with the surrounding cottages. The photograph above shows one of these halls on the eastern side of the city — Moston Hall in 1875. At this time it was owned by the Stingsby family, who had acquired it about 1838 and farmed the land around the hall. The original hall was constructed in the 13th century, but had been rebuilt since then to accommodate the changing fashions of various ages. In the 19th century, the hall was occasionally the scene of the annual Moston Farmers' Rent Dinner. For this event, the local farmers paid 2/6d a head and were entitled to a meal of roast beef, roast mutton and plum pudding. The ale, with which they washed down the meal, was brewed locally and was paid for like the meal. The dinners appear to have been discontinued in the 1890's when urbanisation began to creep on the area after it had been absorbed into the city of Manchester and the part agriculture played in the economy of the area began to decline.

Although the areas on the eastern fringes of the centre of Manchester were regarded as those with the poorest housing and the worst slums, one area in particular claimed to be the worst in the city — the square mile around St. Michael's Church in Angel Meadow. Its narrow packed streets, courts and alleys bred vice and unhealthiness and it was claimed that the largest police station in Manchester, on Rochdale Road, was required to keep order in Angel Meadow. The only open space in that square mile was the site of the old plague burial ground in front of the church which, in 1868, was paved and became known as St. Michael's Flags. Children's swings were erected on the Flags and the open space became a popular venue for Saturday afternoon meetings. Not only did the Angel Meadow area claim to have the worst slums and the largest police station in the city, it also claimed to have the largest lodging house in Manchester. This was a converted cotton mill on Charter St., whose charges varied from 2d to 6d a night depending on the type of accommodation required. The photograph above shows what might be regarded as a typical scene on Angel St., the main thoroughfare through the area and off which ran many of the narrower streets, courts and alleys of the area.

Not only was Manchester the centre of the textile trade with the Royal Exchange, but, during the 19th century it became an important centre of the wholesale trade in south east Lancashire and north-east Lancashire. In 1888 a Royal Commission on markets reported that Salford had no markets worth speaking of owing to the proximity of that town to Manchester and her wholesale markets. In addition to the wholesale markets, there were many smaller markets where members of the public could look and buy freely. One of the most unusual was the Shudehill Poultry Market situated near the junction of Shudehill and Watling St. Here it was possible to buy not only chicken and hens, but also other types of bird — canaries and pigeons for example which could provide a little enjoyment for those in drab conditions. The photograph shows the poultry market around 1895 with one of the many warehouses that were to be found in that area. W. H. Pierce, whose advertisements are clearly visible, started about 1870 and continued to exist until 1901 when it ceased to trade. Pierce's was only one of a number of firms making pipes and tobacco in Manchester at this time which have gradually disappeared over the last 70 years.

As the population of Manchester grew, so also did its dependance on food that had to be brought in from the surrounding areas. The development of the canals in the mid 18th century had further increased this dependance as it was realised that food could be transported relatively cheaply over a fairly long distance to feed the masses. The main wholesale market was Smithfield Market on the eastern fringe of the city centre which enabled the barrow-boys to obtain fresh supplies easily and working classes to buy spoilt produce at lower prices. The photograph above shows the scene outside Smithfield Market in the middle of the 1890's with its boxes and porters. On the right, a greengrocer's shop in one of the suburbs with its poultry and rabbits awaiting purchasers. Every street had either a greengrocers or a grocers of some description. In 1863 there were 17½ columns of shopkeepers in the Manchester directory whilst in 1877 there were 34 columns and in 1902, 38 columns. (Each column averages some 95 names). The local shops enabled those who did not travel into the centre to purchase their needs without having to travel too far from home.

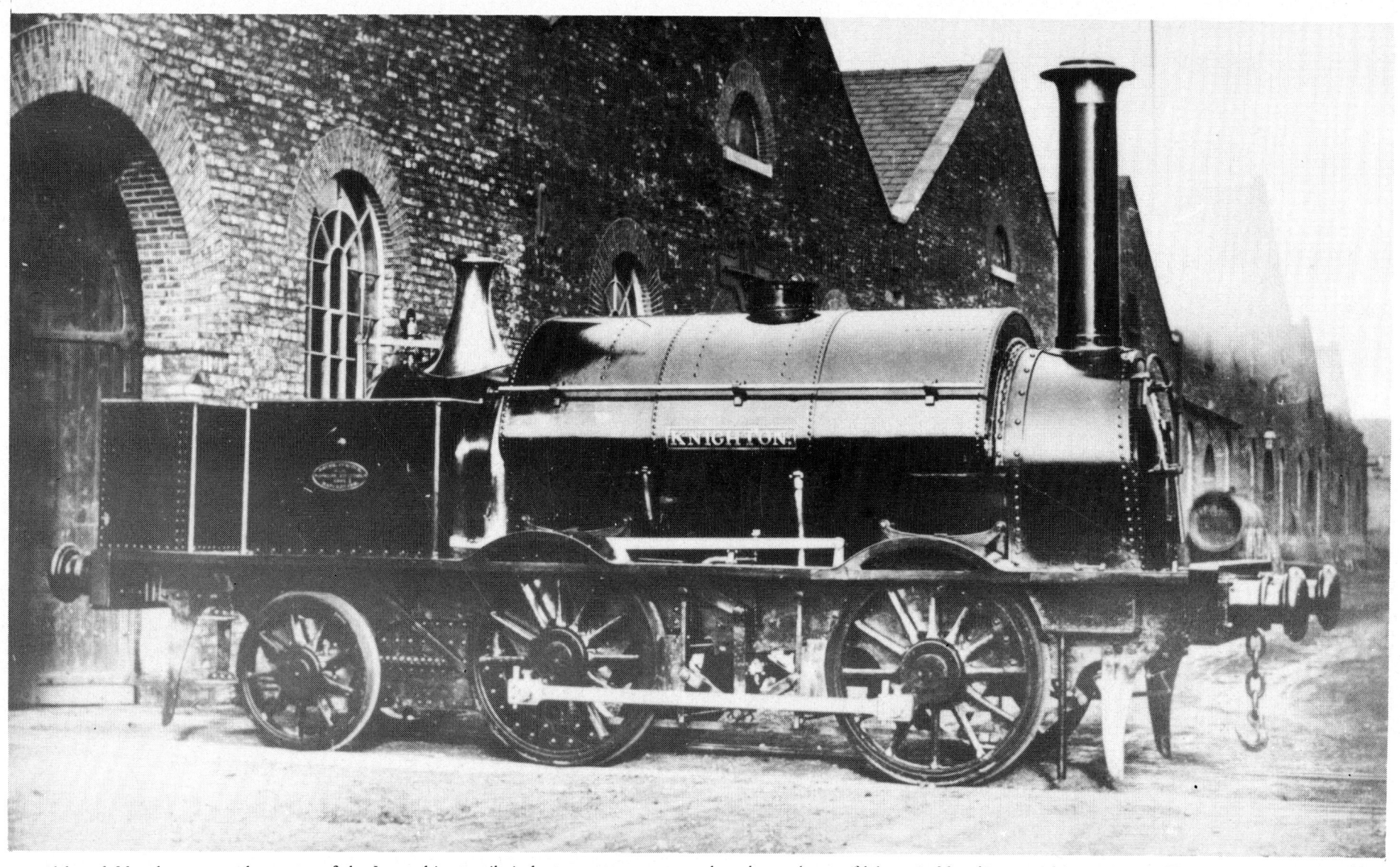

Although Manchester was the centre of the Lancashire textile industry, cotton was not the sole employer of labour in Manchester and its environs. There were many engineering firms who made a wide range of products and amongst these was a firm whose name was to become a household word amongst railway enthusiasts the world over — Beyer Peacock and Co. Ltd. The company was founded in 1854 by three men, Charles Beyer, Richard Peacock and Henry Robertson who invested £25,000 in the company to "make locomotives and other such light machines as the...works are adapted to make". The original site was some 10 acres and this was further increased in 1870 by another 10 acres to accommodate the expansion of the company and prevent it being hemmed in and unable to expand when the right time arrived. The original workshops covered merely 1 acre of the site, but they were laid out in such a way to facilitate additional workshops being added without production being interrupted, which was a forward looking move as several new workshops had to be added within the first 10 years of the company's life and by 1902 there were 9 acres of workshops, linked by a 15" narrow gauge railway. Beyer Peacock's started as a partnership, but in 1883 it became a private limited company and in 1902 it became a public company valued at over £500,000 whose profits in the years 1892-1902 averaged in the region of £63,000. In 1902 the company employed almost 2,000 men and the workshops were said to be capable of turning out 150 engines a year. Such a workshop is shown in the photograph above.

During the 110 years that Beyer Peacock & Co. were involved in the production of railway locomotives, they produced over 8,000 engines from virtually every country in the world. The first order to be received by Beyer Peacocks came from the East India Railway in 1854, but it was the Great Western Railway who received the first locomotives to be made. The reason for this was simply that the Great Western Railway were offering a premium for early delivery, which was an incentive to the fledgling company. Between 1855 and 1858 orders came in steadily and the reputation of the company began to grow. In 1858, P. Stirling wrote "...from the reputation of the firm, I am prepared to receive a first rate piece of machinery". Much of the output of the company was destined for the export market with Holland, East India, Sweden and later Australia, South America and South Africa being amongst the best customers. Locomotives were made for the home market for such companies as the Isle of Man Railway, Great Central Railway and Lancashire and Yorkshire Railway, but their reputation at home was made by their industrial locomotives. The photograph above shows a typical type of industrial locomotive they built. The one depicted is "Knighton" which was built in 1861 for the Knighton Railway at a cost of £1,300, on which the company made 38% profit. In the background the works are visible, a scene that in later works photographs of their products Beyer Peacock had blanked out.

The growth of railways in the middle of the 19th century saw many engineering firms turn to producing railway locomotives. One such firm was Sharpe Stewart, which was also known as Sharpe Roberts, and Sharpe Bros. at various times in its history, whose Atlas Works were situated on the banks of the Rochdale Canal near where it was crossed by Oxford Street. The photograph shows one of the products of that works, Flora, made in 1849 for the Manchester, South Junction and Altrincham Railway. The M.S.J. & A. was opened in 1849 and linked industrial Manchester with rural north Cheshire and turned places like Altrincham and Sale into commuter towns. In 1849 there were 13 trains a day in each direction with the fastest taking 20 minutes and the slowest 30 minutes. Demand was such that by 1885, the journeys had been speeded up and a great many more trains introduced to cater for the demand placed on the line. The M.S.J. & A. was one of the first commuter lines to be opened in the area and was followed by others linking places like Chorlton-cum-Hardy, Didsbury, Heaton Chapel and Crumpsall to central Manchester thus enabling business to get to and from their places of business easily in the same day.

Some of the engineering firms in Manchester remained relatively small employing only a few hands and making a specialist product. The photograph on the left shows the interior of the Midland Iron Works on Travis Street of Henry Gittus. Gittus specialised in the manufacture of punching machines, one of which is shown in the photograph. The first reference to the firm in the trade directory is in 1887 and the last is in 1933.

With horses playing a major part in transport in 19th century Manchester, it was only natural that there should be several blacksmiths operational in Manchester. In 1836, there were 46 blacksmiths and this had risen to 162. The directory for 1900, however, only lists 140 blacksmiths, the advent of the electric tram and the early motor cars were to reduce the number more rapidly in the next decade. The photograph on the right shows Whitehead's Smithy in Rusholme towards the end of the century. Whitehead's had been founded by Thomas Whitehead and another man named Brown around 1845 and continued to function until the mid 1930's. The original smithy was at 80 Wilmslow Road, but as business increased, so additional premises were taken first at 3 and 5 Monmouth Street, Rusholme and then at 546 Claremont Road, Rusholme. In addition to being blacksmiths, Whiteheads were also farriers and wheelwrights, a logical extension of their blacksmiths work.

In a survey made of the manor of Manchester in 1282, it was recorded that the mill on the River Irk, owned by the Lord of the Manor, was worth £17-6-8d a year. This mill had to be used not only by the tenants of the Lord of the Manor, but also the burgesses of the town of Manchester. This situation remained the position until 1758 when Parliament abolished all monopolies on the grinding of corn for bread. The ownership of the mills changed in the 16th century when they were purchased by the Manchester Grammar School to provide revenue to finance its educational activities. Although the 1758 Act abolished the School's monopoly over grinding corm for bread, the Act left the monopoly to grind grain for malt intact. By 1808 this had become so uneconomical that the trustees asked to be relieved of their right, but they were refused. Therefore, they set about improving the efficiency of the mills and were able to raise the profits from £600-£700 to £1,300 by 1815. In 1820 further reorganisation took place when the two mills were merged into a single one and the combined water power of the two mills used for the new mill. Between 1821 and 1836 profits continued to rise and averaged £3,500 per annum. This was, however the high spot for they began to fall so that by 1850 the income from the mills was negligable. The photograph shows that mills on the banks of the River Irk in the mid 1860's with the Grammar School's mill in the centre. (The mill on the extreme right is Phoenix Mill). The site was gradually absorbed by the Lancashire and Yorkshire Railway Company as Victoria Station expanded and the level shown in the photograph is now some 20 feet below the present road level on Victoria Station Approach. Incidentally the footbridge shown in the photograph linking Walker's Croft with Long Millgate still exists under the station.

Textiles were the staple industry for much of south east Lancashire, but it was not the only industry in the area. Manchester had only a minority of people employed in the textile industry. Out of a total population of 543,872 in 1901, only 30,661 males and females over the age of 10 were employed in all aspects of the textile trade in Manchester. Manchester was a late starter in the field of manufacturing cotton because the town had no fast flowing rivers which could be used to drive the machinery and had to wait for the development of steam power to drive machines. Once steam had been adapted to drive textile machinery, Manchester rapidly established its own textile industry, concentrated in the Ancoats area of the city, although mills did exist in other districts. The photograph shows a group of weavers outside a Manchester Mill in the last decade of the 19th century. In 1901 there were 3,772 women engaged in weaving in Manchester and only 382 men. Women, both married and single, made up more than half of the labour force in the textile trade in Manchester with cotton being the most important section of the trade with wool, silk and hemp employing relatively only a few people.

The 19th century saw not only an improvement in the speed by which people could travel from one town to another, but also in the way news and information could be passed. The invention and development of the telephone enabled subscribers to discuss business together without the need for one of the parties to travel or send a messenger to the other party's office or place of business. The Penny Post in 1840 had introduced a postal system into England which became the envy of other nations, but the telephone enabled discussions to be held and decisions made far more quickly than had previously been the case. The tempo of business life was gradually beginning to quicken. The first telephone exchanges were established in Manchester in 1879 by two rival companies, but in 1880 they merged to form the Lancashire Telephonic Exchange and established their exchange in Faulkner Street. By 1881 there were 420 subscribers to the Exchange and expansion rapidly continued. The photograph on the right shows the Switch-board of the Manchester telephone exchange around 1895 with its rows of operators all wearing what appears to be a sort of uniform. The advent of the telephone switchboard provided women with another opening for working in an age when job-opportunities for women were very limited. The arrival of the telephone also altered the sky-line of the city for over business premises there appeared telephone posts with wires stretching across the city. The erection of overhead wires was opposed by the City Council as being unsightly and wanted them laid underground, but it was argued that it was prohibitively expensive and the Council acquiesced in overhead wires when faced with this fact as many of the Councillors were in business and saw the benefits of the telephone and were not prepared to spend more than they needed to.

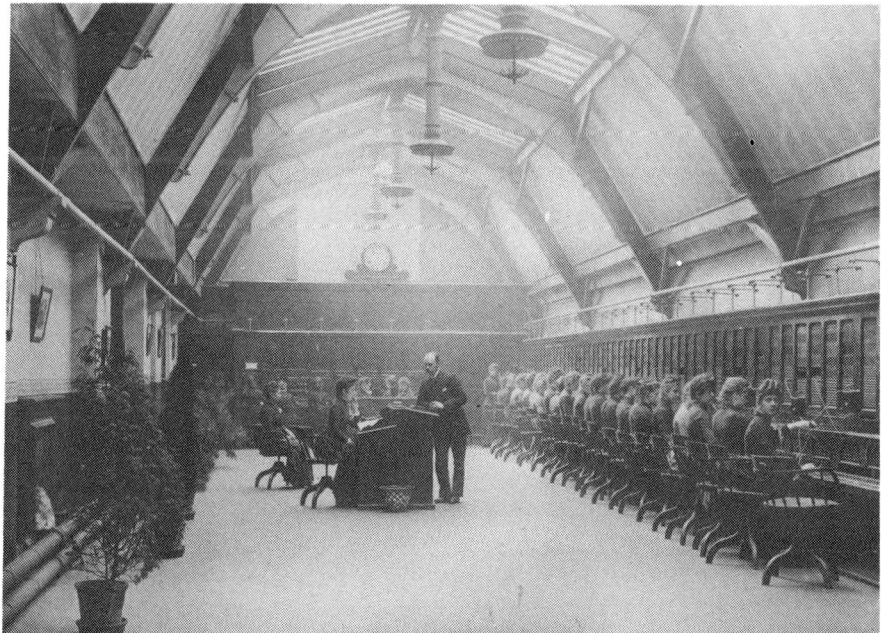

The expansion of Manchester during the 19th century resulted in a demand for houses which meant that there was always a demand for building workers. In 1773, there were only 3,402 houses, but in 1901 there were 108,957 houses and many under construction. For example in 1846 some 1,600 houses were built and another 500 under construction which is a large number for a period when the construction industry did not have the prefabricated methods of the 20th century. The photograph shows a group of Manchester bricklayers at work in the 1890's on a new housing estate in one of the suburbs of the city.

The photograph above shows an elderly cabinet maker at work in his cellar around 1890. At this time, there were many one-man businesses in Manchester some of which were to be found in cellars in the eastern half of the city. Cellars had, until the 1860's been used as shops, but the public health regulations had banned such shops, although only after a long battle. It was, however, much more difficult to ban the use of cellars for other industries and it was many years before effective controls could be introduced. The craftsman shown above was only one of the many who were to be found in the city making not only new furniture, but also undertaking the repair of broken furniture and even doing some general carpentry work to increase their income. Lighting in cellars was virtually non-existant so that it is little wonder that the cabinet maker is wearing glasses.

About 1880 there was founded in Ancoats, the main manufacturing district of Manchester at that time, the firm of Pass and Sparey. During its relatively short existence, the firm established a high reputation for the supply of spindles to the textile trade. Its factory was situated in Vesta Street close to the Ashton Canal and was surrounded by firms of varying sizes. It was, however, conveniently situated to send its products to its customers either by canal, or by the railway, London Road Goods Depot was only a few minutes walk away. The photograph above shows William Pass, one of the owners of the company, with some of his employees in the workshop around 1900. The workers appear to be afraid either of the photographer or of Mr. William watching them during the break to ensure that the company's rules were not broken and as little production as possible was lost. Note the bowler hanging behind the door, a symbol of your station in society when your headwear was determined by your position in the social hierarchy. The firm of Pass and Sparey eventually closed around 1916 due to the effects of the First World War.

East Manchester was the main industrial area of the city of Manchester and contained not only small firms, but some which were large not only in the size of the labour force, but also of the premises they occupied. Many of the large firms started from very small beginnings and grew as a result of hard work and enterprise by their founders. One such firm was founded in 1859 by Samuel Brooks in a workshop in the Union Mill on Minshull Street to manufacture loom temples and small accessories and tools for the textile industry. Demand for the firms products grew so that by 1863 there was a staff of over 60 hands, but even these could not keep pace with the demand. In 1865 the company moved to new premises in Gorton where there was room to expand. Twenty three years later, in 1888, the company took over the Junction Iron Works at Miles Platting to enable production to be increased. Samuel Brooks died in 1886, but demand continued to expand so that by 1900 there were over 600 men employed at the Junction Works and over 1,400 at Gorton. The photograph shows the men at the Gorton works either leaving, or just arriving at, the factory around 1900, but it gives an impression of the size of the work force employed there. The reputation of the company can be shown by the fact that in 1892, a publication called "Progressive Commerce" devotes three closely printed pages to the firm and its products. The Junction Iron Works still stands at the eastern end of Miles Platting Station with a faded notice advertising the firm on the gable wall.

Despite the existence of large factories and mills in Manchester, a certain number of people always preferred to earn their living in the open and independantly of anyone else. Amongst this fraternity, one may count the itinerant musician and the pavement artist, the presence of whom added colour to the life of the day. The top photograph on the left shows a man with his barrel organ touring the streets of Manchester, but he does not appear to be arousing much interest amongst the residents of the street in one of the poorer areas of the city. In fact the only people who appear to be interested in this stranger in the area are the three children around him. More entertaining from the point of view of the public was the musician who had a monkey with him to collect the offerings of the crowd standing around, and to perform a few tricks on the side. The bottom photograph shows just one such musician outside the Lass o' Gowrie public house on Charles Street, Chorlton-on-Medlock. Artists unable to afford a studio or canvas have a ready made supply of material on which to paint — the paving stones with which the city's streets were flagged. The top right photograph shows one such pavement artist at work in front of the Town Hall in Albert Square. Unfortunately, his work does not appear to be attracting any attention from the public, which no doubt disappointed him. Unfortunately the street artist, like the itinerant musician, has long since disappeared from Manchester's streets, leaving the city that much less colourful.

Many factory workers in 19th century Manchester lived close to where they worked and could easily get home for their mid-day meals, but those who did not often took sandwiches to eat at work. However, there was always ice-cream from the carts which could be found in central Manchester. Bottom photograph shows one of the dozen or so ice-cream vendors in Piccadilly around 1899-1900. In the background is the Mosley Hotel which was opened in 1894 and was reported to be one of the "Largest and most commodious hotels in the city". However, it was only the wealthy that could afford to eat in hotels and restaurants in the city centre. Cafes and dining rooms existed in the smaller streets of the city like Charles Roscow's dining rooms at 49 Long Millgate. The dining rooms started out from a boarding house founded in 1874 by Mr. Roscow, which he converted into coffee rooms in 1884 and dining rooms in 1888. Mr. Roscow moved from Long Millgate in 1900. The top left photograph was taken between 1887 and 1893 when Elizabeth King ran a confectionary shop next door. For the newspaper boys and those who wanted a cheap cup of tea or coffee or who could not afford such an item, there was always the coffee tavern run by the Manchester and Salford Methodist Mission in the Central Hall on Oldham Street a few of whose clients have posed for the camera man around 1897 and are shown on the right.

Until the arrival of the internal combustion engine, the motive power road traffic was the horse. Horses were to be found not only on farms, but in the city centres drawing buses, trams and waggons. The result was that every city had its quota of horse dealers. In 1850 Manchester the directory records 8 such people and this had increased to 15 by 1875 and to 17 by 1900. Although these were officially listed horse dealers, no doubt there were very many others who engaged in such activities, especially those connected with farms. In some cases deals would take place privately, but in others the street corner might provide the location for such a deal. The photograph shows the corner of Thomas Street and High Street with a horse being inspected by a prospective buyer whilst those selling it look on anxiously in case any defect be found and the deal falls through. Behind the men involved in selling the horse, a waggon passes with the driver's mate sitting on the back watching the scene as he passes by.

Once a horse had been purchased, there was a wide variety of uses, to which it could be put, not just down on the farm but in other fields as well. The sight of a horse drawn waggon in the 19th century would arouse as much interest then as a motor car does today. The boys in the bottom picture appear to be interested in the drayman loading barrels of beer into the cellar of a public house whilst the horse stands placidly waiting for him to finish his job and move on to the next call. A sign that the horse was the main form of traction is shown in the top right hand photograph where one driver has taken advantage of a horse trough, many of which were scattered throughout the city, to allow his draught animal to obtain some refreshment before continuing to the next place of call. Despite the fact that Manchester was an industrial city, once one left the immediate vicinity of the town, there were many farms to be found. Areas which today are residential suburbs of Manchester all had their farms, the owners of which supplied the local population with fresh milk and other dairy products. The photograph above shows Benchill Farm in what is now Wythenshawe with the farmer ploughing his fields with a horse drawn plough. Wythenshawe had very many farms around 1900 and a glance at the directory lists names like — Baguley Farm, Sharston Hall Farm, Manor Farm in Baguley, and Coxon Farm on Woodhouse Lane. With a large, urban population close at hand, the farmers had a ready made market for their products without incurring heavy transport costs.

During the 19th century, Manchester had living within its boundaries some of the country's most eminent scientists. One result of their presence was the growth of a number of firms making scientific instruments. Often, these firms grew out of opticians who had the skill and machinery necessary for this precision work. In the early 19th century, Charles Joshua Ronchetti, a close friend of John Dalton, founded a firm devoted to the making of scientific instruments. In 1851 a gentleman by the name of Casartelli married into the Ronchetti family and inherited it after the death of its founder. Expansion continued to be achieved until it was regarded as the largest firm of its type outside London with well appointed sales rooms, offices and warehouses. The firm had extensive optical facilities which were regarded as "thoroughly practical and scientific" in their application and paid special attention to dealing with children who had defective eyesight. An off-shoot of the manufacture of scientific instruments was the entry into the field of the manufacture of surveying, mining and engineering equipment, for which there was always a great demand in the greater Manchester area with its very wide range of industries. The growth of the firm forced it to move on several occasions — 1860, 1877 and 1881, each time to larger premises. In 1888 it was described as the "oldest and most important firm of its kind in the city, and indeed has no equal out of London". The firm is still in existance today after over 150 years of activity.

For those who could not obtain regular employment, there were two alternatives open to them: to apply to the workhouse for relief or to make a living the best way they could. One of the ways in which some people chose to earn a living was to collect wood and sticks and to chop it into firewood, bundle it up and to sell it. There was always a great demand for firewood as not only were homes heated by coal fires, but many of the shops, offices and warehouses had fires to provide heat and the easiest way to set the fire going was with paper and sticks. The photograph on the left shows a father with his two sons sitting in either a yard or the street chopping wood into sticks ready to sell to who ever would buy. However, its profitability was always marginal as there was organised competition from the Labour Yard of the Manchester and Salford Methodist Mission.

The poorer sections of the community received a great deal of attention from the various religious denominations that existed in the city. The Manchester and Salford Methodist Mission provided an alternative to the Poor Law for those in need. In the late 1880's, the Methodist church established a mission based on the Central Hall on Oldham Street with the object of helping the people of Ancoats and the other slums of eastern Manchester. In 1891, the Mission opened a home in Hood Street for men who were seeking work, but it was not free — a small charge was made. However, after a month this charge was dropped and the men who took advantage of the facilities worked in the afternoon in a special labour yard either chopping and bundling firewood, handbill distributing, whitewashing buildings, circular addressing or even demolition work. In the 1890's there were average sales of 8,300 bundles of firewood a week and in the year 1899-1900 over 607,000 bundles were sold raising £1,354 to pay for the lodging house. Some people argued that the work the Mission was doing was really the job of the Poor Law Officials, but the Mission argued that their work helped to keep the poor rate down and helped people who would otherwise become chargeable on the rates.

The Manchester and Salford Methodist Mission had a very wide range of activities aimed at helping the residents of the poorer parts of Manchester. Men were the first to be helped and in the annual reports of the 1890's photographs of typical groups of people who were helped by the Mission similar to the one shown above of groups of men applicants. In 1894 the first night shelter for women was opened and the activities soon extended to include girls as well. Amongst the other activities of the Mission were an employment bureau for those seeking work as servants, maternity work was undertaken and those who were released from prison were offered assistance. No accurate figures were kept of those who were assisted, but as its doors were open 24 hours a day it was estimated that over 600 persons were assisted on an average day.

The churches in Manchester were always seeking ways of bringing religion to the masses and encouraging them to become members of this or that particular church. Missions were established in various parts of the city, but the favourite areas were the slums and densely populated areas surrounding the centre of Manchester. The Manchester City Mission was established as the organ of the Church of England whilst the Manchester & Salford Methodist Mission was attached to the Methodist Church. Rather than using buildings, the Missions held open air services in surroundings which were familiar to those who attended. The Methodists often held services in Stevenson Square which were attended by large crowds. On a smaller scale, the Methodists also held services in court yards like the one shown on the left where the residents could attend without leaving their home surroundings. The building in the background is the Jersey Street dwellings in Ancoats and the service was conducted by a member of the Mission Staff. Once a sizeable congregation had been built up, a meeting hall was erected so that people did not have to travel too far to go to church.

The hamlets and villages forming the suburbs of Manchester were not neglected in the movement to evangelise the population and gain new members for a particular church. The United Methodist Free Church used a horse drawn waggon with the message the church was preaching emblazoned on its side. Not only was the message of "Prepare to meet thy God" clearly visable, but also the time of the next service to be held by the "missionaries". The photograph on the right shows the mission car "John Wesley" on a visit to Blackley together with three of the staff of the church who were manning it. In addition to going out to seek new members, the various churches spent much money in building new churches in the expanding suburbs. At the same time older established churches in the central area were having difficulty in remaining in existence. For example St. Mary's church off Deansgate and St. Peter's church in St. Peter's Square had very small congregations and St. Mary's was demolished before the end of the 19th century. In the field of redundant churches, it was the Church of England who suffered most as it was not so easy to close a building and follow the outward movement of population.

In Front of the Royal Infirmary Railings.   Manches

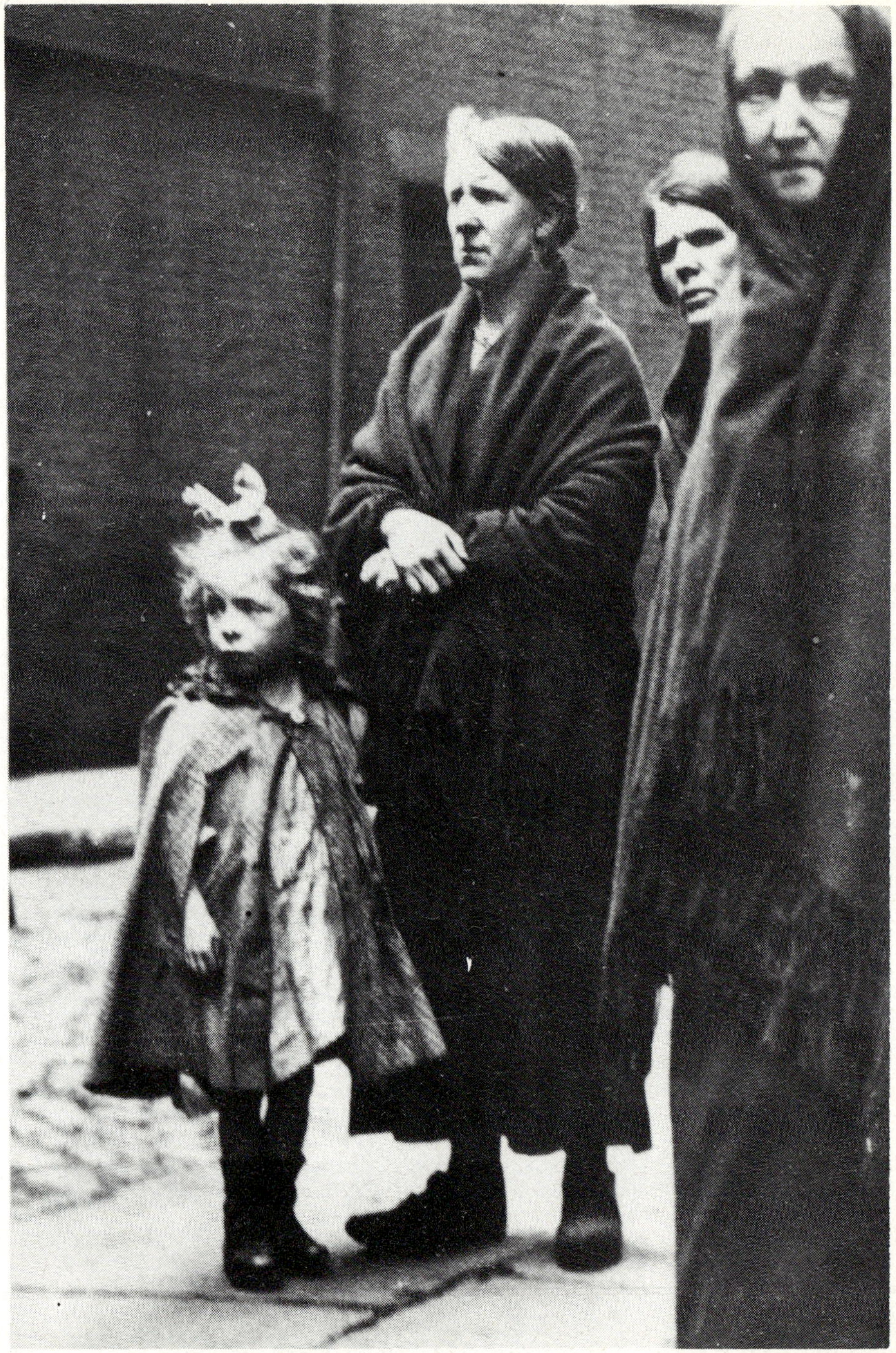

The filling in of the Infirmary pond and the creation of Piccadilly Esplanade in 1853 and the provision of seats along the Infirmary railings provided an ideal gathering place for the public. Those who were shopping in town and visiting a patient in the Infirmary or had nothing to do could sit there and observe the life of central Manchester passing in front of them. In the suburbs, street corners were the usual place where people could gather either to pass the time of day or to discuss prices or the employment situation. The photograph above shows Piccadilly Esplanade about 1897 with some of the people who could be seen there whilst on the right the women standing on the street corner in clogs and shawl, possibly waiting for their husbands to return from work or from looking for a job. Scenes such as this must have been common at times when work was hard to come by.

As central Manchester became more industrial and commercial, so those who could afford to live in the suburbs moved out and commuted to work. This outward movement of the wealthier members of society resulted in the beginning of the bus service in Manchester, but it also resulted in the building of many fine large houses set in their own grounds. It was said in 1862 that no businessman lived in Manchester unless he could not avoid doing so, but most lived at least 6 to 7 miles out and even further. They were encouraged to live in places like Alderley Edge and Altrincham by the railway companies who offered special facilities, as well as rapid transport, into the centre of Manchester. However, in the first decades of the 19th century, the popular places to which the merchant classes moved were closer to Manchester, areas like Cheetham Hill and Crumpsall. The photograph shows the garden of one of the houses in Cheetham Hill with the family having tea on the lawn during summer — an event which those in the densely populated central areas would have never experienced.

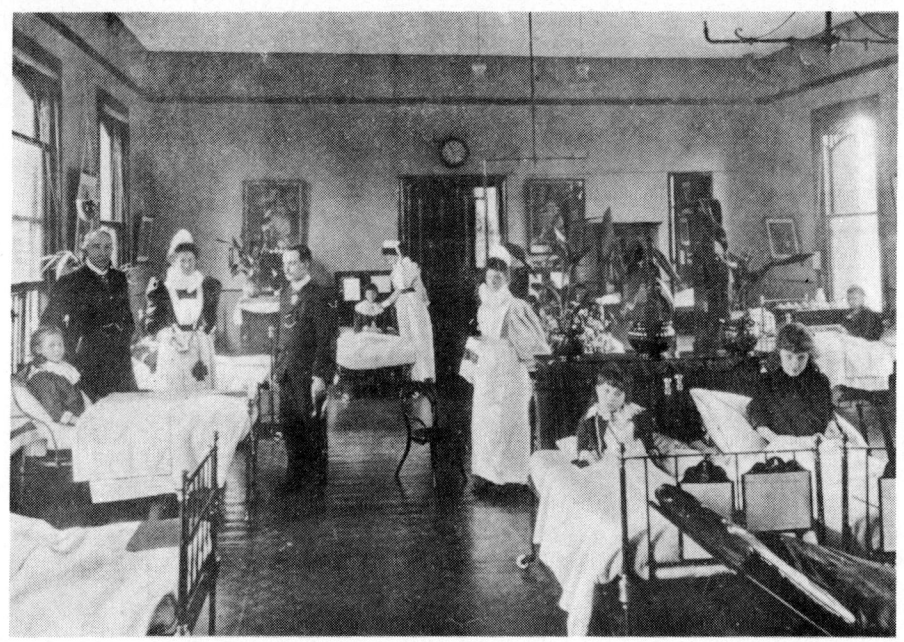

By the middle of the 19th century, Manchester had several hospitals and dispensaries and even a maternity hospital, but there was no hospital dealing specifically with the complaints and illness of children until Doctors Merei and Whitehead took a lease on 8 Stevenson Square in 1856. Here they established a hospital "to provide for the medical and surgical treatment of the children of the poor during sickness and for the maintenance of those whom it is desirable to admit to the Hospital, to provide for the medical treatment of certain forms of disease peculiar to women, and to promote the advancement of medical science with reference to the above mentioned diseases and to diffuse among the operative classes accurate information on subjects relating to hygienic management of children during their early years and to assist in the education and training of women in the special duties of children's nurses". The hospital was situated on the edge of one of Manchester's worst slum concentrations — Ancoats and Angel Meadow, where there was much need for such a hospital. The demand for its services was such that within 10 years, the hospital was forced to move to larger premises. These were in Park Road, Cheetham where there was room for 2 wards each of 12 beds. The residents of the district regarded it as a "haven for the sick poor" with its spaciousness, good lighting and well polished floors. In 1874 and again in the 1880's extensions were necessary so that by 1898 it could offer 60 beds for children and 12 for women. Originally called "The Clinical Hospital and Dispensary for Children", in 1883 its name was changed to the "Manchester Clinical Hospital and Dispensary for Women and Children" in keeping with its wider field of activities.

From the late 16th century until 1834 the problem of dealing and looking after those members of society who were unable to fend for themselves was in the hands of the church, or rather a secular organisation based in the parish. The Poor Law Amendment Act of 1834 altered the whole basis of poor law administration by creating units of approximate equal size called unions. Manchester opposed the alterations claiming that the old system worked efficiently in the town, but after the threat of government intervention, Manchester capitulated. By 1850 the boundaries of the unions in Manchester were established: in the north, the Prestwich Union covered the northern part of the city; the town of Manchester was covered by the Manchester Union; in the south the Chorlton Union covered the area which was absorbed into Manchester in the early 20th century. Each union had its workhouse and staff to administer it. The Manchester Union Workhouse was originally situated in New Bridge Street, but as the site became too small, a new building was erected in the countryside of Crumpsall, a building which was later to become part of Crumpsall Hospital. The Chorlton Union purchased an 80 acre site in 1854 in Withington and there a new workhouse was built which could house almost 2500 persons. The infirmary, shown on the right, was built to a design by Thomas Worthington on principles approved by Florence Nightingale and was mainly used by the old and infirm. The Guardians estimated that the greatest number of inmates of the workhouse were either aged, infirm or widows with children and that winter was the time when the facilities offered were used the most. The diet of the inmates, although monotonous was probably better than those inside could have expected if they had been fending for themselves outside.

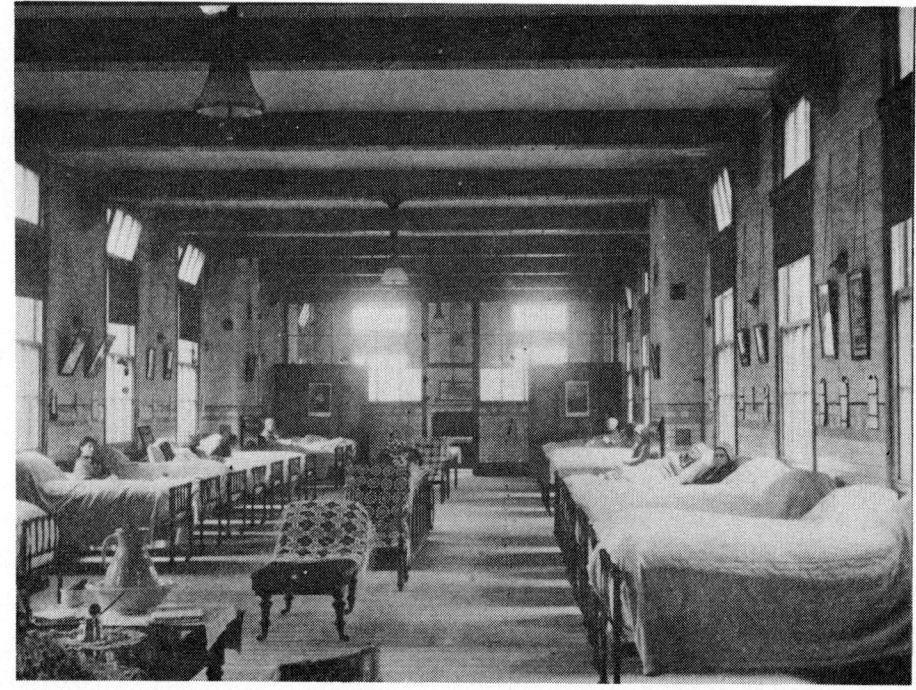

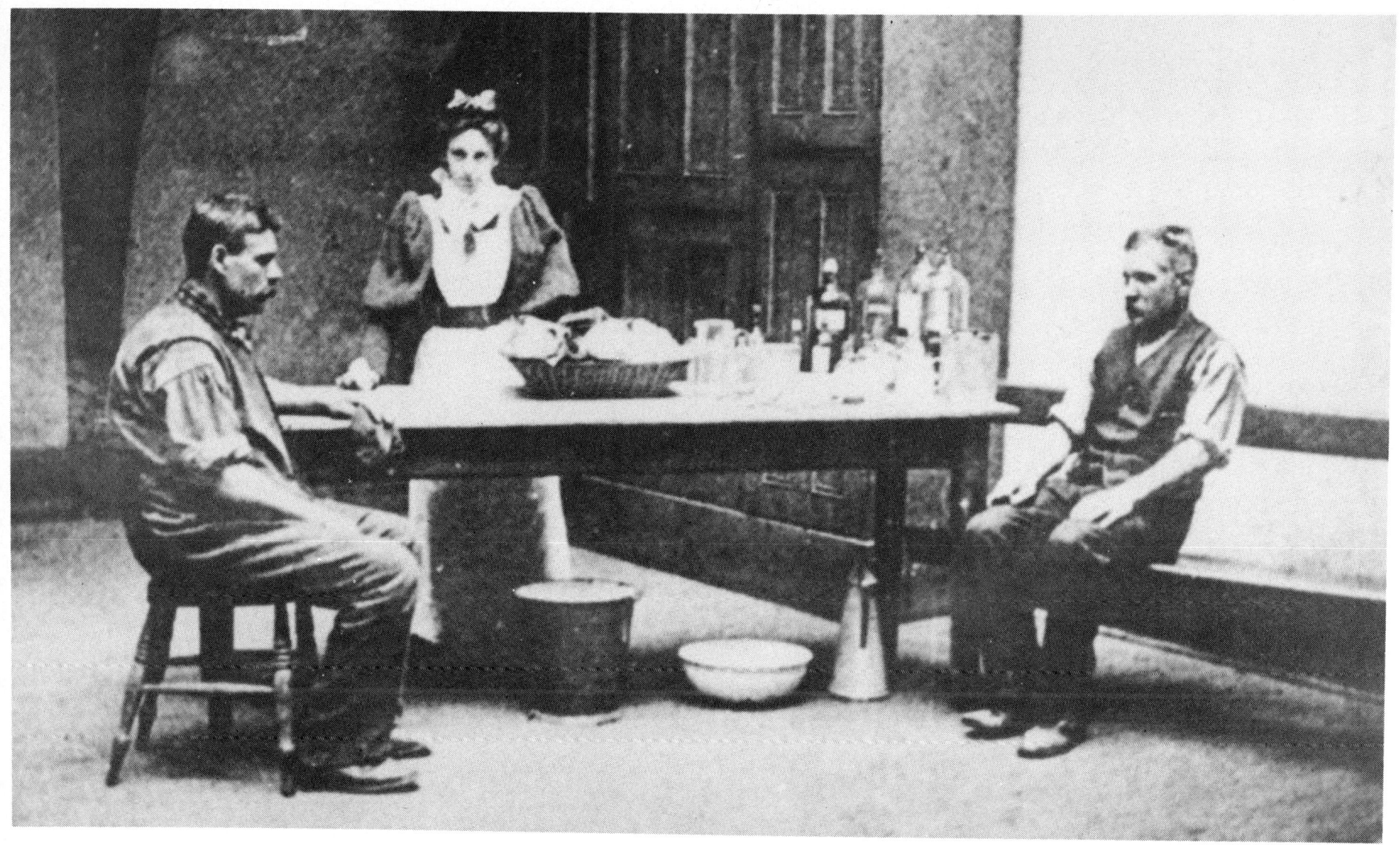

In Victorian England there was no National Health Service to cover a sick person who needed either the attention of a doctor or to go into hospital. If a person was unfortunate enough to be taken ill and need expert treatment, then the fees had to be paid out of the sick person's pocket. In some cases, doctors in the poor areas of the city did waive their charges for the very poor, and probably made it up by increasing their charges to the wealthy who could afford to pay. There was, however, a great need for some kind of outpatient service to the sick and to give advice. In 1869, Edward Weachan established a medical mission to help those in need in the Strangeways area. During the first 25 years of its existence, it treated 73,950 cases as in-patients and the staff gave 74,055 consultations and prescriptions. This showed that there was a need if some type of service could be established. The Manchester and Salford Methodist Mission attempted to fill the gap in the 1890's in the Ancoats area when they appointed a trained nurse to go sick visiting in the area and to hold a dispensary where the sick could attend for advice. During the year 1899-1900, the nurse made 1,800 sick visits to the poor in their homes and dealt with countless cases at the Dispensary which is pictured above. The Dispensary supplied simple remedies, and useful items such as hot water bottles, bed rests, lint, bandages etc., for the people of the area. One one occasion, the Mission's annual report referred to the nursing staff of the Mission in the following terms, which reflect how people regarded those they knew and how they regarded them vis-a-vis doctors:— "The poor folk attached to the Mission have great faith in the skill of the Nurse's concoctions. It is an axiom with them that her remedies are far superior to Doctor's medicine".

The photograph on this and the following page show the scene on Rochdale Road between 1893 and 1898. Rochdale Road was originally called St. George's Road, but in the 1850's it was renamed Rochdale Road on the grounds that it was the main road leading to that town. It was from the Rochdale Road that Angel Street ran leading into the slums of Angel Meadow. The properties lining the road were small, often one man businesses with a preponderance of second, and even third, hand clothes dealers similar to the one on the photograph shown above. At its commencement, Rochdale Road was extremely narrow and traffic congestion caused by this was often criticised. When tram tracks were laid it was found that the road-way was only just wide enough to take a double line of tram tracks. Although schemes were put forward to widen the end nearest the centre of Manchester nothing was done to substantially improve the width of the road or replace the bad housing found there until the railway company wanted to extend its yards and this resulted in some clearance of the worst property found there.

On the previous photograph of Rochdale Road it is not possible to locate whereabouts on the road it was taken, but with the one above it is not only possible to locate whereabouts on Rochdale Road it was taken, but also approximately the date it was taken. The photograph shows the corner of Rochdale Road and Angel Street somewhere between 1893 and 1898 when Steel and Cleaver were the butchers occupying the corner shop – No. 31 Rochdale Road. Previously the shop had been occupied by either chemists or druggists. After Steel and Cleaver had left the premises, the shop continued to be used as a butchers. The family walking down Rochdale Road towards Manchester are passing a wholesale jewellers who occupied both 27 and 29 Rochdale Road whilst at No. 25 where there was an insurance company. In addition to shops like butchers and greengrocers, there were grocers and even a fried fish dealer, a herbalist and a clog maker such as was the variety of occupation practiced in the area by its inhabitants.

One place where the working classes could go for cheap entertainment was the music hall. In 1840 W. Cooke Taylor wrote of the ones he had visited in the area:- "The music was well selected, the songs perfectly unobjectionable, the conversation in some intervals between pieces not only decorous, but to some degree refined and the quantity of the liquor consumed by each individual very trifling". He did admit, however, that other types of music hall did exist giving "crude shows" with "singing, in character, dancing of various kinds, clog and grotesque, juggling, and tumbling by performers especially engaged". Angus Reach visited several music halls during his visit to Manchester in 1849. The audience at the Apollo he described as "decently dressed" and that "several groups formed family parties" and the entertainment consisted of songs and dances accompanied by an orchestra consisting of "two or three fiddles and a pianoforte". In 1853 there was opened in Lower Mosley Street a new Music Hall — the People's Concert Hall, or the Casino. (Popularly it was known as the Cas.) The People's Concert Hall was situated next door to the Gentlemen's Concert Hall and the Quaker's School on a site now covered by the Midland Hotel. Admission prices varied from 2d to 6d depending on where you sat and the hall even boasted boxes which could seat 10 people, although they were often crammed with many more. Amongst the stars who appeared on the stage were Vesta Tilly and Dan Leno, but when the photograph on the left was taken in 1897, it was a cinematograph show that was being held, taking preference over live shows, a sign of things to come. Music halls that were constructed at the end of the 19th century, were, incidentally, much larger and more comfortable than their predecessors catering for all sections of society rather than the artisan and working classes.

In addition to the music halls and concert rooms that existed in Manchester there were also several theatres. Peter Street boasted two of the most popular theatres during the last 25 years of the 19th century and these were located facing each other — the Theatre Royal, which had opened in 1844, and the Comedy Theatre, which had opened in 1875. The photograph on the right shows the second Comedy Theatre, the first, which was opened in 1875, was destroyed by fire in 1883. The replacement building was designed by Alfred Darbyshire in a much grander style than its predecessor for its owner, Edward Gardia. The frontage was 105 feet and could seat approximately 70 in the stalls, 667 in the pit stalls, 200 in the dress circle, 264 in the upper circle and 710 in the gallery. In addition there was standing room for a further 500 patrons giving the theatre a total capacity of almost 2500 places. The building was constructed by Robert Neill in the Venetian Gothic style. The performances that were staged at the Comedy ranged from opera and comedy to burlesque. When this photograph was taken Harry Monkhouse's "Pat" was being performed according to the bills outside. The Comedy Theatre continued to delight its audiences until 1908 when Annie Horniman purchased it to provide a home for her repertory theatre.

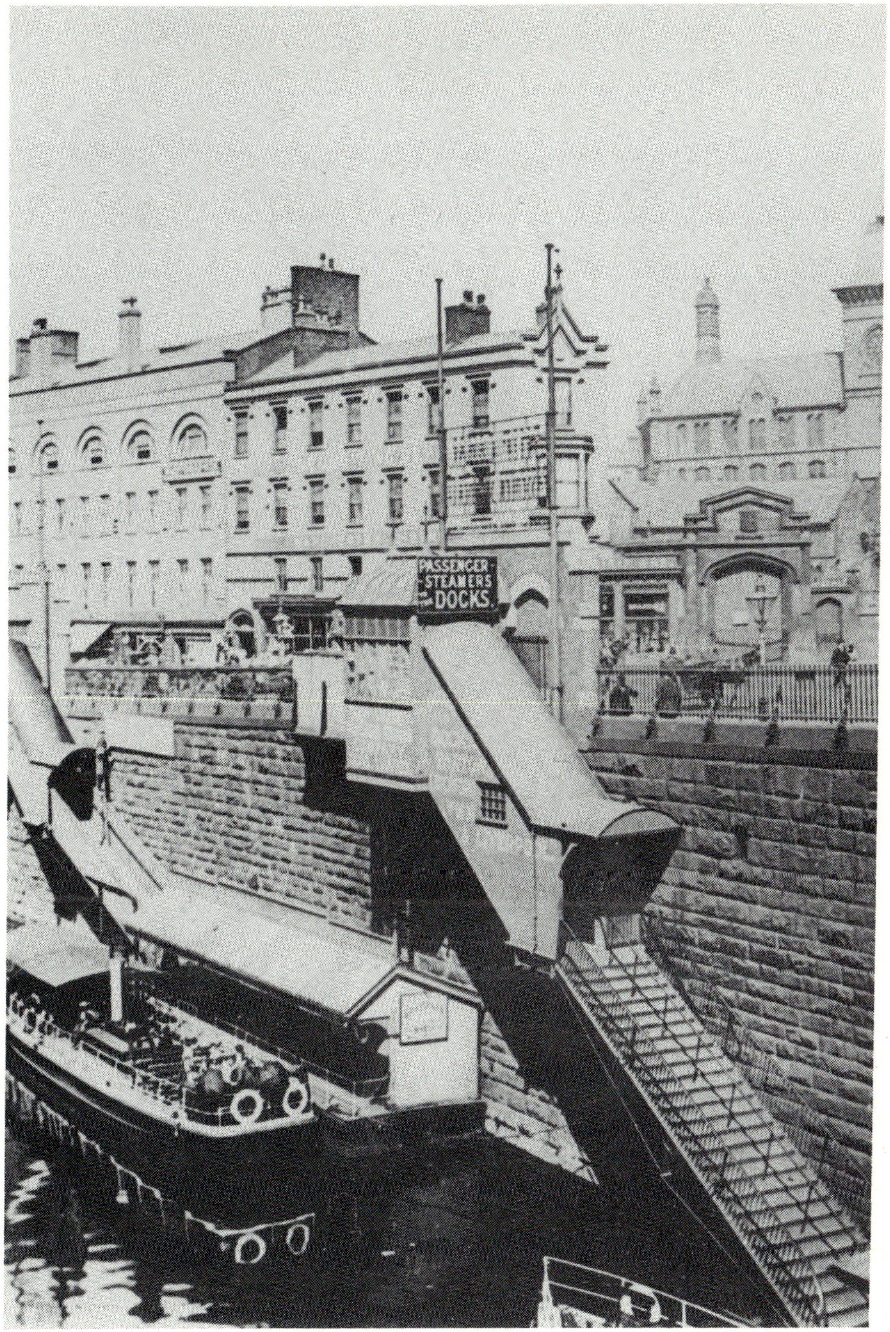

The construction of the Manchester Ship Canal attracted a great deal of attention amongst the people of Manchester and the surrounding districts. When it was finally completed and opened trips were organised along the canal. One could travel from Manchester to Liverpool for as little as 3/6d going one way by rail and the other along the canal. Tours were also organised from Albert Bridge to the docks at a cost of 5d. so that Mancunians could see the ocean going ships in port. The top photograph shows a crowded pleasure boat at Mode Wheel Locks, but it is not recorded whether the passengers had sailed from Liverpool or from somewhere closer at hand. The photograph on the right shows the landing stage on the River Irwell close to Manchester Cathedral which was opened in 1895 as a starting point for trips along the river to Manchester docks and points further along the canal. The Ship Canal Company encouraged this traffic and purchased two steamers, the "Shannon" and the "Eagle" which could carry 900 and 1,100 passengers respectively, specifically for this work. During the first half of 1897 over 200,000 passengers were carried on trips around Manchester docks with the most popular period being the holiday season and public holidays.

One place where a working man could spend his evenings with his workmates or his spare cash at weekends was in the local public house or beer house. Manchester had very many such premises situated not only in the central area where one would expect to find them, but also in the suburbs catering for the residents of places like Levenshulme, Didsbury and Crumpsall. The photograph above shows the Blue Bell Inn in Levenshulme during the 19th century. The licensee at the time the photograph was taken was John Bromiley, but there is no record of the Blue Bell in the directories until the 1930's when the old building was replaced by another one, a modern establishment. The Blue Bell, before it was rebuilt claimed to be one of the oldest pubs in Manchester and after the Rovers Return lost its license in 1928 it claimed to be the oldest in Manchester. Around the door the photograph shows either the landlord's family or a few of his customers, persuaded to leave their drinks for the benefit of the photographer.

The existence of a large number of public houses and other drinking houses and the abuses which existed with young children being given gin and beer regularly gave rise to the temperance movement, which became very strong and influential especially in the large cities. Amongst the arguments against alcohol that the movement put forward were ones similar to the following:—

"Alcohol was responsible for a vast proportion of the poverty, squalor and destitution which makes Great Britain the richest country in the world, also the poorest . . . Drink feeds in our slums . . . It is the chief stumbling block to man's advancement . . ."

Meetings were held in halls and outside factory gates. Temperance bars were established selling soft drinks, tea and coffee and even newspapers and journals published by the temperance movement. The photograph on the right shows a factory gate meeting held by a member of the Lancashire and Cheshire Band of Hope and Temperance Union in the early years of the 20th century. It would be interesting to know the response of the audience and their reasons for attending. Was it an interest in the subject and the dangers of alcohol or was it a chance to do something different during the lunch hour. Not only were factory gates used for meetings, but the movement believed in getting its members young for lecturers were appointed whose job it was to visit schools and explain the aims of the movement to the children and get them to sign the pledge.

A FOOTBALL MATCH AT MANCHESTER.

The lack of public parks and playing fields made it difficult for working men and women to take part in sporting activities either organised or in groups without any organisation. However, they turned out to watch sporting events in their masses as the top left hand photograph shows, at the 1893 Cup Final when Wolverhampton Wanderers beat Everton 1-0 at Fallowfield Stadium. Manchester, at this time, did have two professional football clubs: Newton Heath Football Club, founded in 1885 and which later became Manchester United, and Ardwick Football Club, which became Manchester City in 1894. Neither of these clubs won major honours in the 19th century although Manchester City won the Second Division Championship in 1898-9. For those who preferred less energetic pastimes, a quiet game of cards with friends could pass an hour or two. For the wealthy with their large gardens, private tennis courts could be built where they could play with their friends without being observed by the masses.

In 1844 it was reported that Manchester had "no public park, or other ground where the population can walk or breathe the fresh air and in this respect, is disgracefully defect- ive, more so, perhaps, than any town in the Empire". The situation was partially remedied in 1846 when Phillip's Park was opened, but the shortage of land within the then city boundaries precluded any further parks being created. In 1890 the Trustees of the estate of Sir Joseph Whitworth created a park on the borders of Chorlton-on-Medlock and Moss Side and named it Whitworth Park, after Sir Joseph. The park covered 18 acres and included tree-lined walks, open grass areas, flower beds, a children's park and a lake. For 15 years the Trustees maintained the park and although allowing it to be open to the public reserved the right to close it whenever they deemed it necessary to do so. In 1905, the park was officially handed over to Manchester and was, at that time, the third largest park within the boundaries of the city. During the last decade of the 19th century, the park was open from noon on Sundays until dusk and on weekdays from 8 a.m. until dusk. According to the Manchester Guardian of the 16th June 1890 the park on its opening day was "crowded with visitors" until "the hour the gates were closed". The photograph, taken around 1895 shows the lake and its obvious attraction for the children of the area who were thus provided with somewhere to paddle and sail their model boats on.

The 19th century saw not only the development of a more rapid means of travelling between towns by means of the railway, but it also saw the introduction and development of public road transport linking neighbouring towns and villages. Horse buses had first been introduced in 1824 between central Manchester and Pendleton by John Greenwood, who charged 6d for a single journey. Other routes were gradually established so that by 1862 there were over 60 competing companies. These companies merged in 1865 to form the Manchester Carriage Company, which continued to operate until 1901 when the tramways, as they were by that time, were taken over by the Corporation. (After the introduction of tramways the company changed its name to the Manchester Carriage and Tramways Company.) The original horse buses were drawn by a single horse, but in 1852 a larger vehicle was introduced which required three horses to draw it. Tramways were first introduced in 1877 with the lines being laid by the Corporation and leased to the operating companies for 21 years. The photographs show some of the forms of road transport that might have been seen in late Victorian Manchester. Horse buses continued to operate side by side with the horse trams going to the outer areas. The top left hand photograph shows Mosley Street with a horse bus and the right hand photograph at the top the traffic at All Saints around 1892. Trams occasionally came off the rails and the problem of re-railing was solved by man power rather than by mechanical means as the bottom photograph shows.

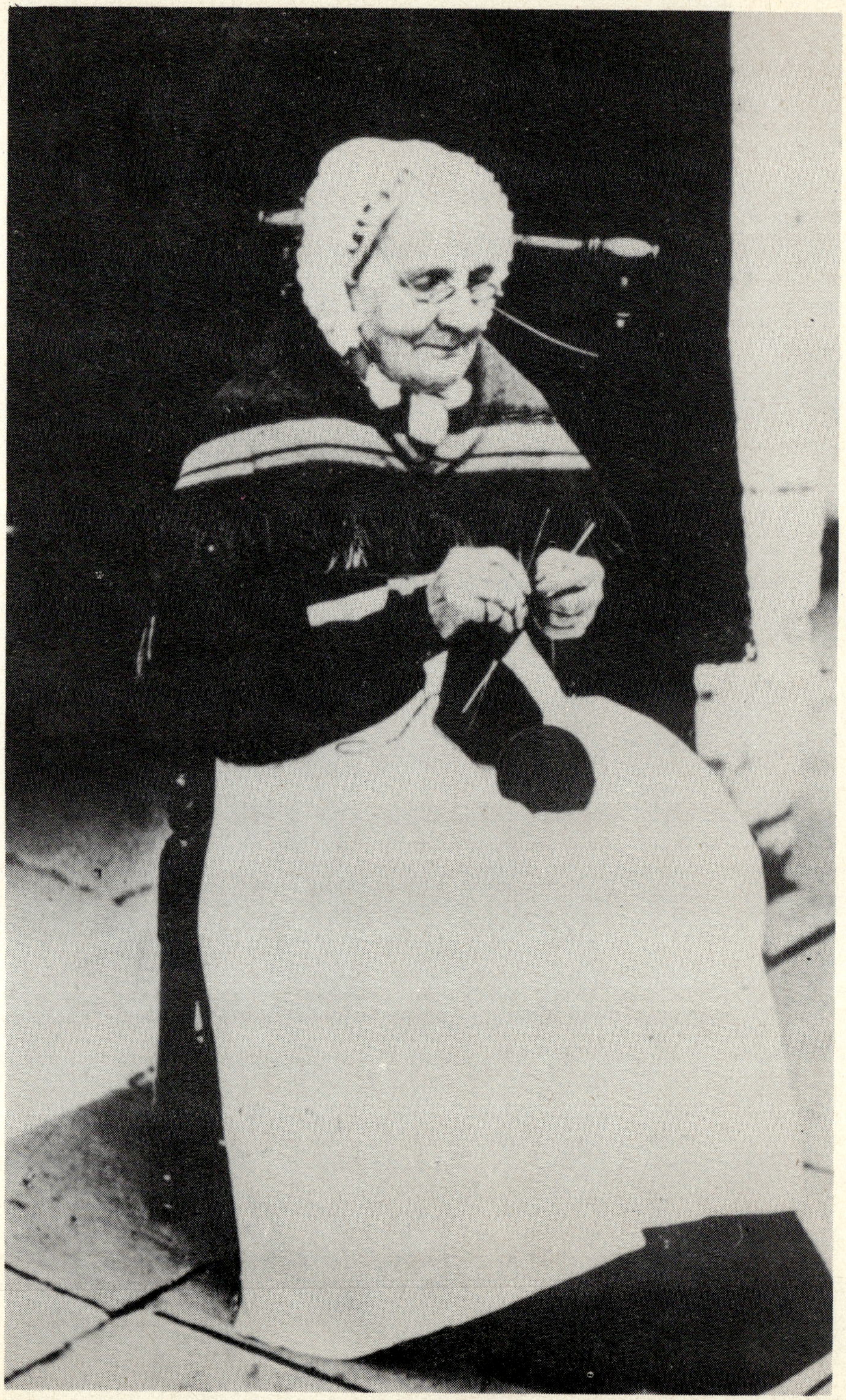

As people grew older in Victorian England, they had no old age pension to look forward to and no old people's homes. They had their savings on which to live and eke out a living. As a result people continued to work as long as possible in order to obtain the best standard of living possible. A quick glance at the occupation tables of the 1901 census will show that there were many who continued to work, especially males, after the age of 65, which would today be regarded as the normal retirement age. For example out of 17,481 recorded as working in the various parts of the building trade 431 were over the age of 65 and in the textile industry, out of 13,502 males employed there, 299 were over 65 years of age. The number of people reaching 65, however, was much smaller than it is today, although people still did reach 90 years and over. In 1901 there were 80 people aged between 90 and 95, 12 between 95 and 100 and one, a woman, over 100 years old. The close knit communities meant that parents and children often lived very close to each other so that the younger generation was always on hand to assist their parents in times of need. If this system broke down and the elderly became destitute or unable to look after themselves and could not afford to pay staff to do, then the workhouse was the alternative. The photograph above shows an elderly man clearing his pipe in his home whilst the old lady on the right sits in the sunshine at her doorstep in Rusholme knitting at the end of the 19th century or the opening years of the present.